Ouch!

Verbal strategies to
support young children

Evelyn Ayum

iUniverse®

OUCH!
VERBAL STRATEGIES TO SUPPORT YOUNG CHILDREN

iUniverse books may be ordered through booksellers or by contacting:

iUniverse
1663 Liberty Drive
Bloomington, IN 47403
www.iuniverse.com
1-800-Authors (1-800-288-4677)

Because of the dynamic nature of the Internet, any web addresses or links contained in this book may have changed since publication and may no longer be valid. The views expressed in this work are solely those of the author and do not necessarily reflect the views of the publisher, and the publisher hereby disclaims any responsibility for them.

Any people depicted in stock imagery provided by Thinkstock are models, and such images are being used for illustrative purposes only.
Certain stock imagery © Thinkstock.

ISBN: 978-1-5320-2126-8 (sc)
ISBN: 978-1-5320-2125-1 (e)

Library of Congress Control Number: 2017905157

Print information available on the last page.

iUniverse rev. date: 04/05/2017

Author's Background

Evelyn Ayum has been an educator for 25 years. She is a Bank Street graduate with a master's degree in reading specialization. She holds an undergraduate degree from Baruch. Evelyn has taught children with disabilities for over 14 years. She is licensed as a teacher of the handicapped, learning disability teacher consultant, reading specialist, supervisor and teacher. She has used the verbal strategies discussed in this book with children from 3 years old to 14 years old for several years. The results were amazing. Children that she has helped use the strategies in this book to verbally defend themselves by using the strategies to stand up for themselves in any situation.

Ouch!

I say **Ouch!** When no one sees or hears me, what can I do? You can go and talk with mom or dad.

Ouch!

I say **Ouch!** When you hurts me by not giving me what I want. Can you make the pain go away by noticing that I am here?

Ouch!

Do not snatch that from me. It hurts my feelings. Tell him that this hurts your feelings.

Ouch!

Can you see the tears in my eyes when you hurt me? I cry when you snatch things from me.

Ouch!

Can you feel the laughter in my voice when everything is okay?

Ouch!

Ouch! let's you know how I feel. I just need to tell you the words that identify my pain before anything happens again. Tell an adult what's happening.

Ouch!

It is my turn now. Can I play with that?

Ouch!

When things belong to me I say these words. "This is my scarf and hat that you are wearing."

Ouch!

Stop hitting me when no one is looking. Touching me where I don't want to be touched. Go tell an adult what's happening to you.

Ouch!

You abuse me and I need the words to tell you to stop. I don't know who to tell. Seek an adult and tell him what's happening.

Ouch!

It is my turn to swing. Please don't make me wait. Use these kind words when it's your turn to do something.

Ouch!

You kicked me and did not say that you were sorry. These are good words for standing up for yourself in any physical situation.

Ouch!

Are there any other words that I can use to express the pain I feel? You can draw your feelings or describe it to an adult.

Ouch!

I was sitting here first. You won't move this hurts my feelings. This is a way to let your friend know that you were seated there first.

Ouch!

You pulled my hair and didn't say sorry. These words let your friends know that pulling you hair isn't right.

Ouch!

I don't like when you say mean things.

Ouch!

You put paint in my hair. Now I am sad and feeling ugly.

Ouch!

It hurts when you say, "I don't want you to be my friend." I want to be your friend.

Ouch!

You ripped my paper
into pieces.
Ouch! I feel angry and
upset!

Ouch!

You stepped on my fingers. It hurts and I feel like crying.

Ouch!

Don't snatch that from me it makes me angry.

Ouch!

Don't pull my clothes or rip them.

Ouch!

You pinched me and that hurts.

Ouch!

I felt embarrassed when you snatched the chair from underneath me and I fell down on the floor.

Ouch!

You knocked me
down and laughed
and I am mad!

Ouch!

Don't tell nasty stories about me. Those stories hurt.

Ouch!

Don't call me names like stupid. I will grow up thinking that I am.

Ouch!

Don't make fun of the way I talk or walk. I have a disability.

Ouch!

I was left at my mom's friend's house all night and didn't eat.

Ouch!

Don't make fun of my name; my grandma had this name too.

Ouch!

I live in a shelter and the noise kept me up all night I need to sleep. These are the words to use to tell your teacher why you need to rest.

Ouch!

I don't hear so well
and I can't see from
far away.

Ouch!

I need a second lunch I haven't eaten all night. My belly is hungry for more food.

Ouch!

Don't make fun of me,
when I'm not looking.

Ouch!

I don't feel well today.
I could have stayed
home but I wanted
to be near my friends
and teachers.

Ouch!

I am wet and need changing. Please don't be mad at me. Can you change me I'm wet.

Ouch!

I am late again today and it's not my fault. Mom had to work all night and got home this morning. Please excuse me.

Ouch!

I know I smell bad but I had to sleep on the train all night. Don't laugh, I am already hurting and not feeling good about me.

Ouch!

My mom and I walked all night, we had no place to go but I am here at school. I am good to go.

Ouch!

My hair is not combed but it's not my fault. Ask an adult to comb your hair for you.

Ouch!

My clothes are dirty and I hurt all over. I am only a little kid can you find me clean clothes to wear.

Ouch!

Do not make fun of the color of my skin or my hair.

Ouch!

I know naptime is over I am tired and sleepy, please let me rest I'll feel better and refreshed.

Ouch!

Don't pretend I am not there when you talk about me to other teachers and parents. I hear your words and they hurt.

Ouch!

I am hungry and my stomach hurts, please give me food to make the pain go away.

Ouch!

I know you can't hear me. I am crying inside. Don't you see the pain in my eyes?

Ouch!

My face is sad and lonely. Can you hold and comfort me.

Ouch!

Maybe tomorrow when you have nothing to do, you can hug me and make the pain that is hurting me go away too.

Ouch!

Then I can feel brand new again with hope in my heart. I now have the words to tell you what's in my heart.

Ouch!

No more hurt, no more days and nights hungry and alone. I have the words to make it all better now on my own.

Printed in the United States
By Bookmasters